DECIDE TO LOVE

A Couple's
Workshop

DECIDE
TO LOVE

Gary and Norma Smalley

with Al Janssen

**Lamplighter
Books** Grand Rapids,
Michigan
Zondervan Publishing House

DECIDE TO LOVE
Copyright © 1985 by The Zondervan Corporation
Grand Rapids, Michigan

Library of Congress Cataloging in Publication Data

Smalley, Gary.
    Decide to love.
    "Lamplighter books."
    1. Marriage—Biblical teaching. 2. Bible—Study. I. Smalley,
Norma. II. Janssen, Al. III. Title.
BS680.M35S64   1985   248.8'4   85-14565
ISBN 0-310-44331-8

Edited by Janet Kobobel
Designed by Ann Cherryman

Printed in the United States of America

85 86 87 88 89 / 10 9 8 7 6 5 4 3 2 1

Contents

Introduction

We are committed to helping build lasting relationships. As a matter of fact, we have dedicated our lives to seeing the family once again become a strong and healthy element in our society. That's why Gary has created seminars, books, and the *Love Is a Decision* film series; they are all designed to equip people, especially married couples, to establish and maintain solid, lasting relationships.

This study book is designed to help further that goal. The emphasis is on application—*on doing,* not just on gaining knowledge. The text, study questions, tapes, and application exercises are tools to help you as a couple open and maintain communication channels.

A husband and wife may complete *Decide to Love* together, but for best results, we suggest that three to five couples study the material in a group. This serves two purposes. First, you will gain further insight into the principles by hearing others share their discoveries and experiences in a supportive environment. Second, the chances of altering habit patterns is greatly increased when there is mutual accountability. Consequently the study is designed with a group in mind. If a couple decides to do the study alone, they should also obtain the *Decide to Love* Leader's Kit, which contains the tapes.

If a group is formed, it works like this: for twelve weeks, each couple will read the introduction and do the Bible study together before the group meets. (The Bible studies are based on the New International Version.) Many lessons also have an application section for the couple. In the group meeting the couples will discuss the study and listen to a ten- to fifteen-minute taped message in which we explain how that week's principle works in our marriage—and why it sometimes doesn't work. Then each couple puts the relationship principles into practice in the Couple Talk section. The group then comes together as a whole to close the meeting. Another important part of the lesson is the Homework. It is designed to help couples apply the relationship principles during the week.

Because this is a couple's study, a husband and wife will work together from one book. We suggest that they take turns writing as they dialogue. The wife might look up the verses while the husband writes the answers, then they might reverse the activities for the next lesson.

For further study and discussion, see the following:

1. The film series *Love Is a Decision.*These six films correspond to the first six lessons in this study. But these lessons are designed to take you much further, helping to make the principles a reality in your life.

2. Books Gary has written:
> *If Only He Knew*
> *For Better or For Best*
> *The Joy of Committed Love*
> *The Key to Your Child's Heart*

The principles you are about to discover have transformed our marriage and our ability to respond to each other. We pray they will be a key factor in how you decide to love your mate.

Gary and Norma

1

Energize Your Mate

After surveying more than 30,000 women across the United States, we have learned women appreciate one specific action when they are frustrated, uptight, nervous, or worried—anytime they are losing emotional energy. Men have a similar need but prefer a different expression to fulfill that need. Knowing what that response is can energize men, women, and children in as little as sixty seconds.

This principle transcends cultural barriers. It works behind the Iron Curtain, in the Middle East, and in Latin America. It's so powerful that it affects the physical growth of children. Some physiologists believe applying this principle can extend men's life spans by two years. These same theorists believe that most women need this response eight to twelve times a day to resist certain diseases caused by stress.

God considers this principle so important that He named part of Himself after it. Let's turn to the Bible to discover what it is.

1. The principle is summarized in 2 Corinthians 1:3–5. Read the passage and answer the following questions:

    a. The key word or principle in this passage is:

b. What is God ready to do for us when we experience trouble?

c. What is our responsibility toward those who are troubled or afflicted?

d. Complete this paraphrase of verse 5:

Just as we experience the sufferings of Christ,

2. We can gain insight into how to comfort by looking at examples of men and women who practiced it. As you look up the following passages, fill out the chart on the next page. Observe the following facts:

a. The person or persons who needed comfort.
b. The problem this person(s) faced.
c. The person or persons who comforted or tried to comfort.
d. The method(s) used to provide comfort.

Passage	a. Person(s) Needing Comfort	b. Problem	c. Person(s) Comforting	d. Method of Comfort
Genesis 33:1–4	Jacob	Esau's army apparently coming for revenge	Esau	embraced and kissed
Genesis 50:15–21				
Job 2:11–13				
Matthew 26:6–13				
Mark 14:32–42	God the Father			
Luke 8:1–3				
Acts 20:17, 22, 36–38				

3. Based on these passages, write a definition of comfort:

4. Whether we mean to or not, we often drain our loved ones' energy. We actually discourage them instead of encouraging and comforting them. We might symbolize this difference by a rock and a pillow. The rock represents how we hurt others and drain their energy. The pillow represents softness, comfort, and encouragement.

Read Ephesians 4:29–32. In the drawing of the rock, write how the passage suggests we could hurt a person who is troubled. Then, in the pillow, list actions and attitudes that the passage suggests might comfort someone.

ROCK   PILLOW

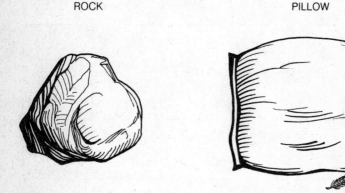

TAPE

Listen to the first section of the tape. We will talk about the importance of comfort and give examples of how it works in our family. Use this page to take notes.

1. One way to comfort is:

2. We all have a tendency to:

3. What we need is:

4. The average wife needs eight to twelve _____ per day.

COUPLE TALK

Spend five to ten minutes talking about how you will apply this principle in your marriage. The wife should start by answering the first three questions. Then the husband should answer the same questions.

1. Think of one situation in the last few weeks in which you received comfort. Describe the situation and how you were comforted.
2. On a scale of 0 to 10, with 0 the worst and 10 the best, how would you rate the comfort you received in this situation?
3. What could have made the comfort more meaningful (if you didn't rate it a 10)?
4. If you have time, clarify this concept by using the following questions:
   a. What form of comfort is most meaningful to you?
   b. How can I tell when you need comfort?

c. What things do I do that drain your energy when you are disturbed?

d. Approximately how many times do you want me to touch you each day?

HOMEWORK

1. Take a 3 x 5 card and write on it a word or phrase that will help you remember this concept. For example, "Don't lecture—comfort" or "Think soft." This will help you remember how to respond when your spouse is discouraged. Mount the card in a visible place, such as the bathroom mirror, the refrigerator, the front door— some place where you will see it several times every day.

2. Schedule an hour now to do Lesson 2 together. Put the date on your calendar. (Do only through Couple Talk, Part 1.)

3. Optional: To further cement this principle into your life, memorize 2 Corinthians 1:3–4.

2

Treasure Your Spouse

Scripture reveals a truth—a treasure—that can raise your sense of importance and strengthen your relationships. This treasure can help you become a better listener. It can make it easier for you to praise others. It can help you stop saying words that hurt those you love.

If you find that there is strain in your home, that you have little desire to attend church, that you aren't even sure you want to do this Bible study, perhaps it's because you haven't found this treasure. If you discover it, understand it, and put it into practice, your positive emotional response will increase in your closest relationships.

Ten clues can help you find this treasure. You may only need one or two to discover the truth. Or you may need all ten. But don't form your conclusion too soon. Diligently examine these verses:

CLUE 1: What does God think about you?

Psalm 139:13–16

Matthew 6:25–26

John 3:16

God thinks I am:

CLUE 2: How should we think about God?

Proverbs 1:7

Malachi 1:6

Matthew 22:37–38

I should give _____ to God.

CLUE 3: What does God think about the environment—His creation?

Genesis 1:31a

Matthew 6:26–29

God's creation is:

CLUE 4: What is the most effective motivation a woman can use to help her husband to accept Christ?

1 Peter 3:1–2

A man finds it hard to resist his wife when she _____ him.

CLUE 5: Why might a man's prayers not be answered?

1 Peter 3:7

What actions described in Malachi 2:13–16 displease God?

The opposite of acting violently is:

CLUE 6: What could cause God to curse an entire nation?

Deuteronomy 28:15–20

Malachi 2:2

Obedience to God's laws is a sign of:

CLUE 7: What might be one reason why some people live longer, are more successful, and have fewer problems in life?

Ephesians 6:1–3

Children who obey their parents are demonstrating:

CLUE 8: How does God want us to position ourselves in relation to others?

Philippians 2:3–8

The best example of this attitude is:

CLUE 9: How does God want us to view marriage?

Hebrews 13:4

Adultery weakens a marriage because:

Have you discovered the treasure? Write a word or phrase that summarizes how we're to view God, His creation, other people, and our family:

If you are not sure, here's one more clue. . .

CLUE 10: Read Romans 12:10. The second half of this verse tells us to _____ each other.

Many symbols in our world illustrate this concept. Match the symbols in the right column with the appropriate relationship in the left column:

1. Worshiping God
2. Appearing before a king

3. Man and his future wife
4. Waiter's respect for a customer
5. Employer recognizing employee's contribution
6. Most valuable player on an athletic team
7. Appreciation of a major customer
8. Wife's birthday

☐ **A.** Diamond ring
☐ **B.** "Yes, Sir" and "Yes, Ma'am"
☐ **C.** Bonus, raise, or praise
☐ **D.** Kneel

☐ **E.** Dozen roses

☐ **F.** Special discount

☐ **G.** Bow

☐ **H.** Trophy

COUPLE TALK (PART 1—DO THIS PART BEFORE THE MEETING)

Our priorities are a reflection of what we value most. The following is a list of possible priorities. Choose ten of them that are important to you as individuals, not necessarily as a couple, and list them on the chart on the following page. In the second column, the wife should list what she perceives is the value of that priority, using a number between 0 and 10, with 10 representing the highest possible value. In the third column, the husband writes a number between 0 and 10, indicating how he values that priority. Then discuss what you both feel the desired value should be. When you come to an agreement, put that number in the final column. If you can't agree, then put the average of your two numbers.

Sample of *Priorities*

Job	The Bible
Husband	Friends
Wife	Reading
Children	Time alone, doing nothing
Money	Resting
Hobby (list specific one)	Cooking
TV	Sleeping
Church activity	Eating
Sport or recreation	Cleaning
God	Phone conversations
	Other (specify)

Priority	Wife's Actual Value	Husband's Actual Value	Desired Value
1.			
2.			
3.			
4.			
5.			
6.			
7.			
8.			
9.			
10.			

TAPE

Honoring one another is of tremendous importance in marriage; failure to understand and apply this principle will cause trouble in the home. Listen to the tape as we relate how we discovered this crucial concept could work for us. Use the following page for your notes.

1. To honor or value a person means to:

2. Honoring your mate is a _____, not a _____.

3. On a scale from 0 to 10, with 10 the highest, indicate where you would rate God, your spouse, your children, yourself, and your job or career:

0 _____ 10

COUPLE TALK (PART 2)

Few objects are more valuable than diamonds. Richard Burton once paid $1.2 million for a 69-carat diamond that he gave to Elizabeth Taylor. The Tiffany & Co. once put a $5 million price tag on a rare, canary-yellow diamond. The Hope diamond is considered one of the world's most valuable gems. But to a woman who is just engaged, her diamond ring is equally valuable, not necessarily in dollars, but because of the meaning she attaches to it.

The key to honoring your mate is to realize his or her incredible value. Below are drawings of large diamonds. One is for the husband, the other for the wife. Answer this question: "My mate is valuable because _____." Fill in each space of the diamond with an answer. You may want to take turns sharing qualities, or you may each complete your diamond and then share all the qualities at once.

WIFE   HUSBAND

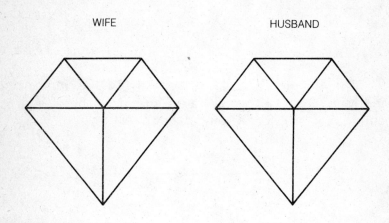

HOMEWORK

1. Do something this week to demonstrate how highly

you value your mate. Husbands, you may want to bring your wife a rose, or you could arrange for a baby-sitter and take her to her favorite restaurant. Try to be creative and think of something special you haven't done in a long time.

2. Schedule now to spend an hour doing Lesson 3 together (through Application) this week.

3. Optional: Choose one of the verses studied in this lesson and memorize it.

3

From Disharmony to Reconciliation

In counseling husbands and wives, parents and children, employers and employees, coaches and athletes, we have observed one major cause of disharmony and conflict. This problem often results in deep resentment, bitterness, and sometimes complete collapse of the relationship.

We have observed that as people apply the principle in this lesson, their relationships can be restored and made even stronger than before the conflict—even in "hopeless cases." One wife was so distraught that she shook at the mention of her husband's name. Within six months they were back together and more in love than at any other time during their twenty-five years of marriage. The principle of open and closed spirits was the key to their reconciliation.

To help us understand this concept, let's look at two relationships in the Old Testament:

David and Michal
Absalom and David

DAVID AND MICHAL

David and Michal's relationship began when David was a young man, shortly after he defeated Goliath. One of the "spoils" of his victory was to marry one of King Saul's daughters (1 Samuel 17:25). Saul wanted to give David his daughter Merab (1 Samuel 18:17). But David refused, saying, "Who am I that I should become the king's son-in-law?"

1. Read 1 Samuel 18:20–29.
   a. Describe Michal's feelings toward David:

   b. David viewed his marriage to Michal as (mark the statements you think apply):

   _____ A challenge

   _____ Something that was expected

   _____ The natural result of his love for her.

   _____ A chance to improve his relationship with the king.

2. Read these four other passages that refer to Michal:

   1 Samuel 19:11–17
   1 Samuel 25:39–44
   2 Samuel 3:13–16
   2 Samuel 6:16, 20–23
   a. Describe how Michal felt about David in 2 Samuel 6.

b. Check which of the following factors may have contributed to her feelings:

☐ She felt David never loved her.

☐ She regretted having helped David escape from Saul.

☐ David never called for her when he was in the wilderness.

☐ David forgot her and married Abigail as well as several other women.

☐ She was jealous of the love the public had for David.

☐ David demanded her back without considering her feelings.

☐ She realized David was greater than her father and resented it.

☐ She didn't believe in God.

☐ David had no sympathy for Paltiel, Michal's second husband.

☐ She was experiencing menopause.

☐ David made no effort to mend their relationship.

☐ David was more concerned about political impressions than her needs.

DAVID AND ABSALOM

Because of David's many marriages, the relationships of his children were adversely affected. His daughter Tamar was raped by her half-brother Amnon. Humiliated, Tamar spent the rest of her life secluded in her brother Absalom's home. Because of the rape, Absalom hated Amnon and, two years later, succeeded in a plot to kill him. Pick up the story by reading 2 Samuel 13:30–15:12. This passage begins with an erroneous report to King David that Absalom had struck down all of his brothers.

1. After reading the passage, check the reasons you think Absalom rebelled against David:

☐ David took too long to call Absalom back from his exile.

☐ David favored Solomon over Absalom.

☐ David would not see Absalom after his return from exile.

☐ David never forgave Absalom's murder of Amnon.

☐ Absalom was bored.

☐ The people of Israel propelled him to power.

☐ Absalom was jealous of the love people had for David and wanted it for himself.

2. Michal and Absalom are examples of people who closed their spirits. Based on these illustrations, what do you think it means to have a closed spirit?

Do you agree or disagree that (circle "Agree" or "Disagree"):
David could have changed Michal's heart.
     Agree   Disagree

David could have kept Absalom from rebelling.
Agree   Disagree

APPLICATION

1. Read Matthew 5:23–24 and check the statement that most closely agrees with these verses:

☐ If I offend someone, but that person also offended me, I should wait for the other person to make the first move.

☐ No matter who was wrong, I should make the first move.

☐ If I offend someone, I'm responsible for seeing that the matter is cleared up between us.

☐ If I offend someone, but that person says "forget it," then everything is fine.

2. If you are offended, how do you feel when:

a. The person who offended you says and does nothing?

b. The person who offended you tries to justify his or her actions?

c. The person who offended you asks for your forgiveness?

3. If you knowingly offend someone, how do you feel about your relationship when:

a. You say nothing and hope the other person will forget?

b. You argue that the other person was wrong too, but he or she doesn't admit it?

c. You seek the other person's forgiveness and try to restore the relationship?

TAPE

Listen to the tape as we discuss this concept and illustrate how it works in marriage and family relationships. Use this page for your notes.

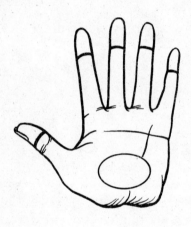

How can we be reconciled to another person? Another way to phrase that question is to ask, "How can I open a person's spirit?" We have found five steps that work in most cases. The steps don't have to be taken in a particular order. To help remember them, we compare them to opening a fist, with each finger symbolizing a step toward opening that person's spirit.

Step 1, thumb:

Step 2, index finger:

Step 3, middle finger:

Step 4, ring finger:

Step 5, small finger:

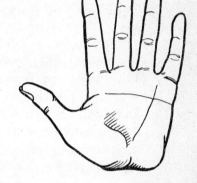

COUPLE TALK

The following list describes ways that a person can close the spirit of his or her mate. Ask your spouse to choose one item on this list that he or she feels you have done recently:

1. Ignored you.
2. Didn't value your opinions.
3. Showed more attention to other people than to you.
4. Didn't schedule special time to be with you.
5. Didn't give you a chance to voice your opinion before making a decision.
6. Made jokes about you.

7. Came back with quick retorts.
8. Spoke harshly to you.
9. Lectured you when you needed to be comforted.
10. Told you how wonderful others are but didn't say how special you are.
11. Showed disrespect of your family and relatives.
12. Didn't praise you for something you did well.
13. Didn't show interest in your personal growth.
14. Didn't occasionally tell you, "I love you."
15. Failed to spend time with you when you were at a party.
16. Showed more excitement about work or other activities than about you.
17. Didn't help with the children.
18. Didn't volunteer to help with dishes after a meal.
19. Made you feel stupid when you shared an idea about his or her work.
20. Criticized physical and emotional characteristics you can't change.
21. Spent too much money and got the family too far into debt.
22. Didn't tell you how important you are.
23. Forgot special dates like anniversaries and birthdays.

Now ask your spouse the following questions:

1. How specifically did I close your spirit?

2. How did it make you feel when I said or did that? (Seek to understand.)

3. How much did this close your spirit? (You may have your mate mark on the line on the following page to indicate how much he or she perceives that the situation closed the spirit.)

open   completely closed

4. Follow the five steps (remember the finger exercise) to help reopen your mate's spirit.

HOMEWORK

1. Repeat the Couple Talk exercise at least one more time this week.

2. On a 3 x 5 card write a word or phrase, such as "Open hand, open heart" or "Open spirit," to help you remember this principle. Place the card in a conspicuous spot.

3. Schedule time to do Lesson 4 together (up to the Tape section).

4. Optional: Memorize Colossians 3:12–13 or Acts 24:16.

5. Optional: If you watch TV together this week, look for times when someone closes another person's spirit. (Some shows have numerous instances of this. The more you recognize it happening to someone else, the easier it will be to recognize it in your marriage and to reduce the times you close your mate's spirit.)

4

Nurture Your Marriage

When our family lived in Illinois, we planted a large garden every spring, and all the plants seemed to thrive in the rich soil. Every fall, we enjoyed a bountiful harvest of corn, tomatoes, squash, peas, and beans.

Then we moved to Texas. The soil in our back yard was sandy. We were advised to fertilize it with rotten cotton hulls, so we bought a huge bag, tilled it into the soil, and planted the garden.

The okra and corn thrived. The tomatoes looked perfect—at first. But as they ripened, the bottom halves rotted. The beans grew to about four inches, then they withered. When we pulled up the carrots, they were mushy.

We had two choices. We could say to our plants, "Shape up or we'll pull you out by your roots." Or we could find out why our plants were sick and make some corrections. Of course, we chose the latter. Our investigation revealed that the fertilizer had made the soil too acidic, and we needed to add a neutralizer. The carrots couldn't handle the hot sun and needed a protective net over them. The beans needed more water. When we made those adjustments, we were nurturing our garden. Much like gardeners tend their plants, we need to nurture our marriages.

1. Read Ephesians 5:21–33.

a. What is God's highest aim for husbands (verses 25–27)?

b. In your own words, state what you think these verses mean today:

c. Paul amplifies this idea in verses 28–30. He says that a person who loves his body _____ and _____ for it, just as Christ does His church.

Some translations use the word *nurture* here. It comes from the Greek word *ektrepho,* which means "to promote health and strength, to 'bring' up or promote growth." The Latin word *nūtrīre* is similar. It means "to feed, suckle, provide the necessary ingredients for growth and well-being." A person who nurtures someone is much like a plant lover who takes time to discover what a plant needs and then does whatever is necessary to meet those needs.

d. List five ways you take care of your body:

e. What insight does this give you into caring for your mate?

f. From whose example in this passage can we learn how to love and nurture our mates?

2. To understand how to nurture, we need to understand how Christ cares for His church. We will examine first His care for His disciples, then His examples and instructions recorded in Acts and the Epistles.

Read each passage in the chart that starts below and observe the following:

a. How Christ loves His church or one person within it—look for one activity or principle.

b. How this applies to the husband—look for one or more present-day applications.

c. How this applies to the wife—look for one or more present-day applications.

Verse	How Christ Loves Church	Husband's Application	Wife's Application
John 17:1,6,9	Pray for her	Pray for wife	Pray for husband
Mark 6:30–31			
Mark 14:3–6			

Verse	How Christ Loves Church	Husband's Application	Wife's Application
John 11:33–36			
John 13:12–17			
John 14:27			
Acts 2:44-45			
Rom. 5:8			
Rom. 8:38–39			
Phil. 2:5–8			
Col. 3:13			
2 Thess. 2:16–17			

TAPE

The principle of nurture is practical. It means *meeting your mate's needs*. Listen as we explain how it works. Use the outline on the next page to take notes. You will need the notes for the Couple Talk that follows.

Four Basic Needs of Women:

1.

2.

3.

4.

Five Basic Needs of Men:

1.

2.

3.

4.

5.

COUPLE TALK

1. Men, on a scale from 0 to 10 (with 10 the highest), rate how you feel each of your five main needs are being met. Then women, select the need that you think is the least volatile and ask your husband how you can move it closer to a 10. After he's answered, repeat the answer: "Do you mean you would like me to . . . ?" Once you understand, go on to number 2 in the Couple Talk.

2. Women, on a scale from 0 to 10, rate how you perceive each of your four basic needs is being met.

Take the least volatile one and suggest what it would take to move it toward a 10. Husbands, paraphrase your wife's suggestion until she agrees that you understand what she's saying.

3. Try to recall your wedding vows. Or ask your Bible study leader for a copy of the traditional wedding vows. Answer these questions:

a. What does the husband promise his wife?

b. What does the wife promise her husband?

c. Why are witnesses present when you make these vows?

d. What implications do those vows have for you now?

4. Consider renewing those vows to each other now or sometime soon. You could do this with your Bible study group as witnesses.

HOMEWORK

1. Repeat the Couple Talk points 1 and 2 at least once this week, with each of you talking about another need you perceive.

2. Schedule time to do Lesson 5 together (through Couple Talk, Part 1).

3. Optional: Start a "How God loves us" chart. As you read the Bible in family or personal devotions, observe every instance in which an aspect of God's love for us is revealed. Your chart should have two columns. In the left column, write down how God loves us. In the right column, put any application you see for how you should love your spouse. Put the chart in a prominent location.

5

Close-Knit Families

Write a paragraph describing one of the most memorable childhood activities you did with your family or another family.

Husband:

Wife:

Share your paragraphs with each other. As you do, you may discover the secret of close-knit families.

1. Imagine yourself in the upper room with the disciples after the resurrection and ascension of Christ. Pentecost had not yet occurred. Read Acts 1:12–14. What does the writer find significant to report about this group?

2. Read Acts 1:15–23. What was required of the person who would take the place of Judas and become one of the twelve disciples?

Imagine the discussion the disciples and the women may have had during a meal break in this prayer meeting. Surely they must have reminisced about the many things Christ taught them. They probably also spent time recalling some of the events they shared together. Let's examine five incidents from that perspective. As you read these passages, try to put yourself in the sandals of the disciples.

3. Read Mark 5:1–20.

a. Describe the situation from the disciples' point of view:

b. What do you think they felt?

c. What did they learn about Christ through this experience?

4. Read Matthew 12:1–8.
    a. Describe the situation the disciples faced:

   b. How do you feel when you are criticized (especially when the criticism is unjust)?

   c. How do you think the disciples felt when the Pharisees criticized them?

   d. How do you think the disciples felt after Christ rebuked the Pharisees?

5. Read Matthew 14:22–33.

    a. Describe the situation the disciples faced:

    b. How do you think the disciples felt, first when they battled the waves, then when they saw Christ coming to them on the water?

    c. What did they learn about Christ through this experience?

6. Read Mark 14:26–52.

    a. If you had been Peter, John, or James, describe what you might have felt and thought as you waited in the garden for Jesus:

    b. Describe the events that took place after Jesus prayed:

c. What do you think the disciples felt as they saw their leader arrested?

7. Read Luke 24:1–33. Choose one of the following people: Mary Magdalene, Peter, John, or Cleopas. Describe that person's day in detail. What was that person thinking at dawn? What was he or she feeling? How did he or she first hear the news? What was that person's first reaction? How did he or she respond when the risen Christ appeared?

8. After recounting the experiences in questions 3–7, how do you now feel toward the disciples as they are in the upper room in Acts 1?

9. Check the ingredients you think contributed to their sense of oneness:

☐ They were all fishermen.

☐ They had a common goal.

☐ They came from the same town.

☐ They spent three years together.

☐ They experienced common struggles.

☐ The crises they endured came from outside sources.

☐ They all loved Jesus Christ.

COUPLE TALK (PART 1)

Discuss what ingredients would make your next vacation or family outing a 10. Write each of your ideas down:

Husband:

Wife:

TAPE

The factors that contributed to the disciples' oneness can also draw a family together. We will explain. Use this page for notes.

1. The key to close-knit families is in maximizing _____ and minimizing _____.

2. The secret to close-knit families can almost always be found in this activity: _____.

3. Closeness does not necessarily come _____ _____ but _____.

COUPLE TALK (PART 2)

1. Examine the suggestions in Couple Talk, Part 1. Plan a vacation or family outing that would include as many of these suggestions as possible, while keeping within your budget. (Note: If you have older children, it's important to include them in this process, too.)

2. Discuss what activities you can share together as a family this next week. Be specific. Here are some ideas:

Church
Picnic
Participatory sports event
Bible study
Helping others
Game night

Note: It's better to have activities that *involve* everyone. Avoid passive activities, such as TV or movies, that allow for little interaction.

HOMEWORK

1. Schedule at least one family activity that every member would enjoy this month.

2. Schedule time to do Lesson 6 together (through Application).

6

Secret to Fulfillment

People want the same basic things in life. To love and to be loved. To be content. They seek contentment by trying to earn enough money, knowing the right people, finding the perfect home, or simply discovering their niche in life.

For many people, those strivings prove fruitless. Even when they achieve their dreams, they often find no lasting fulfillment. This study reveals what we believe is the secret to a consistently fulfilling life. We believe anyone can experience lasting love, joy, and peace regardless of circumstances. To find out how, start with a brief personal evaluation.

PERSONAL EVALUATION

1. When were you worried recently?
Husband:

Wife:

2. What caused you to worry?
Husband:

Wife:

3. When were you angry recently?
Husband:

Wife:

4. What made you angry?
Husband:

Wife:

5. When were your feelings hurt recently?
Husband:

Wife:

6. What caused your feelings to be hurt?
Husband:

Wife:

7. Check which of the following you have experienced in the last six months:

☐ envy
☐ jealousy
☐ fear
☐ lust
☐ discouragement
☐ depression
☐ loneliness

8. Choose two of the emotions you checked and write what you think were the causes of each:

Husband: emotion:

        cause:

        emotion:

        cause:

Wife: emotion:

        cause:

        emotion:

        cause:

9. Negative emotions generally are caused by people, places, or things. Look over the causes of your emotions and organize them on the chart.

Causes of Negative Emotions

People	Places	Things

BIBLE STUDY

1. What word or phrase summarizes what has robbed you of fulfillment? Write it in Box 1 of the flow chart (see page 58). Colossians 3:2 and 1 John 2:15 may help you find the answer.

2. What assurances do the following verses give us?
   a. John 12:23

   b. John 15:11

   c. 1 John 4:7

   d. What or who is the source of each assurance? Write this in Box 2 of the flow chart.

3. Read Ephesians 3:14–21.
   a. With whom and what does the apostle Paul want us to be filled?

   b. Read 1 John 5:9–15. To be filled with all that God desires for us, it is imperative that we first

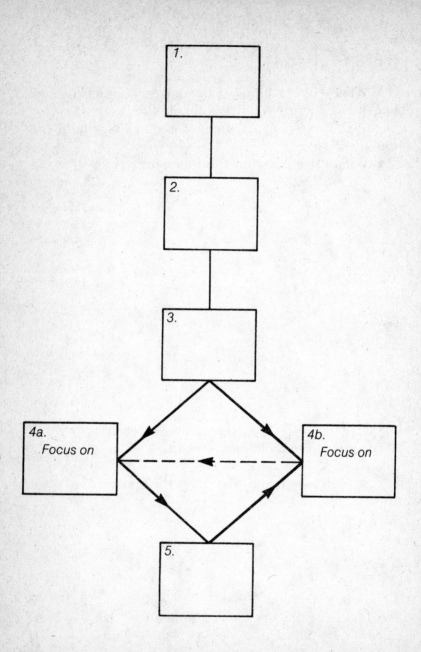

1.

2.

3.

4a.
Focus on

4b.
Focus on

5.

_____

_____. Summarize this (from verses 12 and 13) in Box 3 of the flow chart.

4. Unfortunately, even after we experience God's love through Jesus Christ, we still struggle with our old desires. We do not experience constant fulfillment. Our lives are not constantly full of love, joy, and peace.

   a. Read 1 John 2:15–17. The reason we often continue to experience negative emotions is because our focus is on the _____. Put your answer in Box 4a of the flow chart.

   b. Read Philippians 3:7–10. Paul considered all of his earthly accomplishments to be _____. Instead, his focus was on _____. Write this second answer in Box 4b of the flow chart.

5. How does one move from 4a to 4b? Read 1 John 1:9 and write your answer in Box 5 of the flow chart.

APPLICATION

1. Share with each other where you are on the flow chart. Is this where you want to be? If not, where do you want to be? Discuss how you can help each other establish and maintain your focus on God.

2. Write out a prayer of either:

   a. Initial commitment to Christ, or

   b. Redirecting your focus from the world back to Christ.

Husband:

Wife:

TAPE

Listen to the tape and use this page for notes.

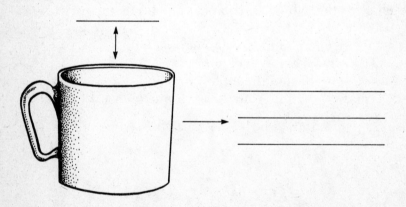

1. We should not look to God's _____ to provide what only the _____ can give.

2. When God fills your cup, everything else you might gain is:

3. The key to a fulfilling life is:

4. The purpose of wrong emotions is to reveal:

COUPLE TALK

1. Share with each other one goal or dream that, if it were fulfilled, would make your cup overflow .

2. Pray together for each other's dreams.

HOMEWORK

1. Repeat your prayer of focus on Christ at least once every day.

2. Schedule a time to do Lesson 7 (up to the Tape section).

3. Optional: Memorize Ephesians 3:19–20.

7

New Appreciation

Prospecting is still a popular activity in the Pacific Northwest and Alaska. Prospectors dip a pan into a mountain stream, filling it with gravel and water. Then they swirl the material, gradually dumping the gravel until all that remains, they hope, is one or more gold nuggets.

We need to learn to pan for gold in our relationships, sifting through what we see as negative traits and circumstances to find the gold nuggets. In fact, every circumstance that we think is cause for bitterness and anger in our lives actually contains the key to a richer, more fulfilling Christian life. But discovering the gold may require us to make decisions that are contrary to our nature.

Our tendency is to notice unusual or undesirable behavior in others. If a boy puts away all but one of his toys, his mother may scold him for forgetting that one, without thinking to praise him for the others he put away. A person can often point out the one or two things wrong with a meal, never thinking to compliment the cook for the effort taken to prepare it.

1. Think of at least one situation in the last few weeks in which you experienced anger or resentment. Identify who sparked the emotion and then answer the following questions:

Husband:

  a. The person who touched off my emotion was:

  ☐ spouse   ☐ child   ☐ boss   ☐ other

  (_____)

  b. Describe the situation:

  c. What emotions did you experience as a result?

  d. Try to explain why you felt that emotion:

  e. What did you do about it?

  f. Can you think of one benefit from this situation?

Wife:

  a. The person who touched off my emotion was:

  ☐ spouse   ☐ child   ☐ boss   ☐ other

  (_____)

b. Describe the situation:

c. What emotions did you experience as a result?

d. Try to explain why you felt that emotion:

e. What did you do about it?

f. Can you think of one benefit from this situation?

If you couldn't think of a benefit from the situations, don't feel bad. That is something you can change with practice. But first it helps to understand *why* we should look for the good in negative situations.

2. What are God's two greatest commandments (Matthew 22:37–40)?

    a.

    b.

3. What three things are God's will for us in all circumstances (1 Thessalonians 5:16–18)?

    a.

    b.

    c.

On a scale from 0–10, with 10 representing "always," mark where you think you are in fulfilling the commands in questions 1–2. Mark "H" for the husband, "W" for the wife:

        0 _____ 10

On a scale from 0–10, with 10 being the highest, mark how much you believe it's possible to experience these things in your life.

        0 _____ 10

Write about one situation in which you find it difficult or impossible to practice these commands:

Husband:

Wife:

4. Read Romans 8:28–29 in the New International Version and fill in the blanks:

"And we know that in _____ things God works for the _____ of those who _____ him, who have been called according to his _____."

a. Describe one situation in which this has proved true in your life:
Husband:

Wife:

b. Describe one situation in which this has *not* appeared to be true in your life:
Husband:

Wife:

c. Based on verse 29, what is God's purpose for our lives?

d. Describe one way that the situation in *"b"* has helped to fulfill the purpose stated in verse 29?

Husband:

Wife:

5. Read Hebrews 12:9–11. Why does God sometimes discipline us?

6. Read James 1:2–5,12. List at least two benefits of suffering:

TAPE

Perhaps you are familiar with the passages you just read. The question is not if they are true, but how they work in your particular circumstances. Listen as we share how God has made this principle real in our lives. Use this and the following page for your notes.

How to praise when you endure trials:
  1.

2.

3.

4.

Emotions come:

GROUP DISCUSSION

Discuss the following as a group, filling out the chart as
you go. In the left column are listed some qualities that
are often considered faults. In the right column, write
how that fault can be expressed in a positive way.

HOW TO PRAISE A SPOUSE FOR HIS OR HER FAULTS

Fault	Positive expression
Manipulating	Resourceful, with many ideas and creative ways to manage people.
Touchy	Sensitive, which is helpful in raising children.
Nosy	
Stingy	
Talkative	
Flighty	
Too serious	
Too bold	
Rigid	
A dreamer	

Fault	Positive expression

Overbearing

Too fussy

COUPLE TALK

The following chart may help you discover gold. In the first column write something you like about yourself, about God, and about a person you struggle to get along with (friend, neighbor, co-worker). In the second column, write something you dislike. And in the third column, think of one benefit of that trial (makes you more patient, teaches you how to love, helps you learn how to be kind). Try to think of more than one benefit for each trial.

	Like	Dislike (Trial)	Gold: Benefit
HUSBAND:			
about self			
about God			

	Like	Dislike (Trial)	Gold: Benefit
about _____			
WIFE:			
about self			
about God			
about _____			

Write a one-sentence prayer, thanking God for the gold you have discovered.

Husband:

Wife:

HOMEWORK

1. Write in bold letters on a 3 x 5 card a word or phrase that will remind you to praise your mate and children. You could write, "Praise" or "Gold" or "Talk Positive." Put the card in a conspicuous spot.

2. Make it a point to praise your mate at least once every day this week.

3. Schedule time to do Lesson 8 together (through the Practice Session).

8

Change Behavior— Painlessly

What would cause a man who had consistently offended his wife in an area for twenty years to completely stop that offensive action and never repeat it again? It was something his wife said, and it only took her five minutes.

That same technique, taking only ten minutes, helped a husband motivate his wife to stop criticizing and condemning him each night when he got home from work.

It's a communication method that is thousands of years old, but its unique power has only been rediscovered by our generation. Roman Catholic church leaders use the concept in their marriage encounters. They call it "dialogue." We call it "emotional word pictures."

Throughout the Old and New Testament, emotional word pictures were used to teach truths and to bring people to repentance.

1. Read 2 Samuel 11.
   a. Summarize the situation:

b. What do you think was David's attitude about his sin (verses 25–27)?

2. Read 2 Samuel 12:1–14.
    a. Summarize Nathan's word picture:

    b. Describe David's emotional response to the story (verses 5–6):

    c. Based on David's response, what did Nathan do (verse 7)?

    d. What was the result (verse 13)?

    e. Based on Nathan's example, try to define what an emotional word picture is:

3. Jesus was a master at using word pictures. In fact, it was one of Christ's primary teaching tools. He used word pictures in His parables, His similes ("The Kingdom of God is like . . ."), and His metaphors ("I am the Bread of life").

A good example is Christ's Sermon on the Mount. In the following passages, identify the word pictures and the messages you gain from them:

Verses	Word Pictures	Message
Matthew 5:14–16		
Matthew 6:19–21		
Matthew 6:25–27		
Matthew 7:3–5		
Matthew 7:24–27		

4. Read James 3:1–12. Identify at least seven word pictures in this passage:

a.

b.

c.

d.

e.

f.

g.

h. What message do you gain from these verses?

i. How do the word pictures help you understand this message?

PRACTICE SESSION

Choose a color that fits your mood right now. Share it with your mate. Be as detailed as possible. For example, if you say green, is it a dark, forest green or a bright green like a freshly mowed lawn?

TAPE

Listen as we share how this principle can be applied in communication between husband and wife. Use this page to take notes.

How to use word pictures:

1. Use _____ statements.

2. Decide on the _____ you want to communicate.

3. Choose a word picture that is either:
   a.

   b.

c.

4. If it doesn't communicate:

5. Another way to help communicate is to:

COUPLE TALK

Choose an object in the room where you are sitting. Use a word picture to describe how you feel about your marriage relationship in terms of that object. After you have given your word picture, your partner should try to understand the picture better by asking you questions. The goal is to visualize and enter into each other's life as much as possible.

HOMEWORK

1. Describe how you feel about either a problem or something exciting in your family. Or describe an internal emotion or conflict you are experiencing. The following is a list of ideas from which you might draw a picture:

You are a train—where are you, or where are
                 you heading?
          a car—what condition are you in?
          a flower—describe what kind, color,
                 and condition.
          on a path . . .
          up a tree . . .
          in a boat—describe the size, kind, and condi-
                 tion of the sea.
          in a war . . .
          in a cave . . .
          on a mountain . . .
          an item of clothing . . .
          a rug . . .
          a piece of art . . .
          the weather . . .
          an animal—what kind are you? Are you free or
                 caged?

Give as much detail as possible. If your partner feels
your picture is not clear enough to understand, have
him or her ask clarifying questions.

2. Schedule the time to do Lesson 9 together (through
the Junior Course).

9

A Degree of Wisdom

The Bible suggests one thing you can do that guarantees you will be considered wise. Not only will you receive wisdom, but you also will gain honor, praise, and respect. By gaining this one thing, this "diploma," you will also gain God's power to love your mate, children, and neighbors. God says that to love Him and others is His highest command, but we can't do that satisfactorily in our own strength. However, if you earn this diploma, you will lay the foundation for receiving God's power.

To earn this degree, you need to successfully complete at least four courses, an internship, and, of course, a final exam.

FRESHMAN COURSE

1. Circle one: I   *a. like*   *b. don't mind*   *c. dislike* being criticized.

2. Look at the following verses and indicate what qualities God considers necessary if a person is to be wise:

Proverbs 1:5

Proverbs 3:7

Proverbs 9:8–9

3. What do the following verses suggest is the difference between a fool and a wise person?

Proverbs 10:14

Proverbs 12:15

4. Why would it be to your benefit to seek out criticism?

SOPHOMORE COURSE

1. Read Hebrews 12:5–11.

a. What do you see about God's discipline in this passage?

b. What are some ways that God reproves us?
Proverbs 1:28–33

Matthew 18:15–17

2 Timothy 3:16–17

JUNIOR COURSE

1. What do the verses on the following page teach about the benefits of heeding reproof as well as the consequences of ignoring it?

2. What is God's evaluation of the person who hates reproof or correction (Proverbs 12:1)?

	Heeding Reproof	Ignoring Reproof
Proverbs 10:17		
Proverbs 13:18		
Proverbs 15:32		
Proverbs 29:1		

SENIOR COURSE (TAPE)

Listen now to the tape. Use the following outline for notes:

1. Why seek correction?

2. Where do the desire and energy come from to make corrections?

3. Who can give me the best correction?

4. Use the sandwich approach to criticism.

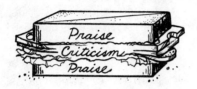

5. Other approaches to criticism:

INTERNSHIP (COUPLE TALK)

To graduate, you must complete an internship; it's your Couple Talk for this lesson. The husband should go first, then the wife. Follow this outline:

1. Ask your spouse to discuss one area in which he or she feels you need improvement (i.e., spending time together, raising the kids, making household repairs, managing money).

2. Gently help your spouse explain the feelings and thoughts he or she has about this area.

3. Paraphrase your spouse's ideas and ask if your version explains his or her feelings and thoughts. It may be necessary to paraphrase the ideas and feelings several times before you completely understand.

4. Encourage your spouse to use word pictures to help you understand. For example, "When you ignore me at a party, I feel like a house plant with its leaves yellowing and drying up" or "When you yell at the kids, I feel as though all of us are bushes that have been sprayed with poison."

5. If you uncover deep hurts or frustrations, try to *understand* how much your spouse hurts. Be sure to ask for forgiveness.

6. Do not react, criticize, or justify yourself. If you do, you will probably not continue to receive help in becoming Christ-like.

FINAL EXAM

Write out a paragraph on the following page, stating in your own words your commitment to accept reproof. Try to include the following elements in the paragraph:

1. Why you are willing to accept reproof.

2. Areas in which it may be difficult to accept reproof.

3. People you will ask to give you reproof.

4. People from whom you would find it hardest to accept reproof.

5. What area of your self-perception is most threatened by reproof (i.e. masculinity, femininity, intelligence, objectivity).

HOMEWORK

1. If you have children, schedule a few minutes during or immediately after dinner for a family council.

a. Each member of the family should give some words of praise about every other family member.

b. Allow each child to give Mom and Dad a word of advice about something he or she would like to see you do or change to make home a better place to live.

2. Schedule time to do Lesson 10 together (up to the Tape section).

3. Optional: Memorize Proverbs 9:8–9.

10

24-Hour Protection

All meaningful, growing relationships have some degree of give and take. Each person experiences periods of highs and lows. A husband may be discouraged because he lost a promotion, because a six-pound bass fell through the bottom of his net, or because his wife continually fails to respond to his sexual advances.

A wife may lose emotional strength because of her menstrual cycle. Or she may have heard that her best friend is moving. Or she just may have put a large scratch on the side of the new car. She may be driving a car that frequently breaks down. She may be frustrated because no one seems to understand the pressure she's under just before dinner. She may feel consumed by the unending responsibilities with the children and her own vocation.

It's at times like these that a husband or wife can do one thing that not only will be a tremendous encouragement to the other person but also will strengthen the relationship.

1. Read 1 Thessalonians 2:7. What analogy does Paul use to convey the love he has for the Thessalonians?

The word translated "caring" or "cherishing" comes from a Greek word that means "to warm" as a mother bird would cover her young in the cold or rain. It's similar to the concept of nurture—finding and meeting the needs of another. But the word "cherish" also conveys the idea of protecting. We can sometimes express love to our mates and children by protecting them in situations in which they are vulnerable.

2. Read the following verses and match each passage with methods God, Jesus Christ, or someone else used to cherish. Some passages contain more than one method. You may write down additional insights under the references.

1. Deuteronomy 32:7–14	☐ **A.** Removed the physical danger in a life-threatening situation.
2. 1 Kings 1:1–4	☐ **B.** Provided desperately needed medical attention.
3. Mark 4:25–41	☐ **C.** Provided protection while in dangerous territory.
4. Luke 8:1–3	☐ **D.** Showed incredible concern for one group's benefit.
5. Luke 10:30–35	☐ **E.** Displayed sensitivity to not give people more than they were able to handle spiritually.
6. Romans 9:2–3	☐ **F.** When one method didn't work, sought another to keep this person comfortable.
7. 1 Corinthians 3:1–2	☐ **G.** Provided needed resources for the ministry.

In the house, draw a picture of your mate doing some activity that demonstrates your spouse cherishes you. Don't worry about the quality of the drawing—stick figures are fine. After each person has had a chance to draw a picture, repeat the exercise. Discuss your picture and explain why you appreciate your mate's action.

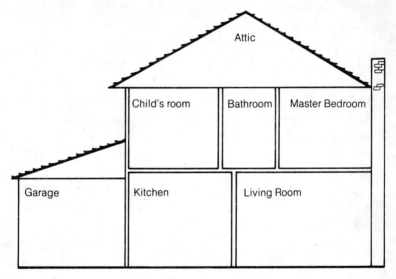

TAPE

Listen as we explain what it means to cherish your spouse. Use this outline for your notes.

1. To cherish means to:

2. Specific ways to cherish your spouse:

a.

b.

COUPLE TALK

Ask each other one or more of the following questions. When appropriate, use the tools you've already learned (comfort, word pictures, and praise) to help your discussion.

1. What are some of your personal struggles and frustrations?

2. What potential conflicts or dangers are you facing?

3. What help do you need in battling some unwanted habit?

4. What pressures am I causing you?

5. What personal goals have you not achieved? What can I do to help you fulfill those goals?

HOMEWORK

1. Select one area from your Couple Talk in which your mate could use your help or protection. Plan a specific way to help this week without telling him or her.

2. Schedule time to do Lesson 11 together (through Application).

3. Optional: Memorize Ephesians 5:29.

11

Sure-Fire
Attention Getter

True or false? You can lead a horse to water, but you can't make it drink.

If you answered true, think again. Suppose you dump a lot of salt in the horse's oats? Do that, and you probably couldn't stop the horse from drinking.

Few things are more frustrating than trying to communicate information to someone who's not interested in listening—it's like trying to make a horse drink. Wives throw up their hands as they try to talk to their husbands who prefer to read the newspaper or watch TV. Getting youngsters to be still long enough to hear what you have to say may seem impossible. Husbands can be frustrated trying to talk to their wives about the car or his job.

But you can get a person's attention any time you want to and hold it for as long as you need by using the Salt Principle. Jesus Christ was a master at it.

1. Read Luke 15:1–2 and take note of the chaotic situation. A crowd gathered around Jesus. Among the group were some religious leaders who were grumbling and telling everyone that Jesus associated with the wrong kind of people. It was a situation that could quickly get out of hand.

If you were in that situation, which of the following options do you think would get the crowd's attention:

☐ Shout, "May I have your attention please!"
☐ Ask the disciples to forcibly remove the Pharisees so you could speak.
☐ Call up someone to sing special music.
☐ Threaten, "If no one will listen, I'm going to another town."
☐ Start to explain why you welcome sinners and eat with them.
☐ Arouse the crowd's curiosity.
☐ Get several sports and entertainment figures to endorse you.
☐ Other

2. Read Luke 15:3–4. Note that Jesus started speaking by using a word picture. But He added a twist—He asked a question.

   a. Why would Jesus use such a word picture?

   b. Why did He ask a question instead of immediately stating His point?

3. Read Luke 15:8–10.

   a. Why would Jesus use this word picture?

   b. Why did he begin by asking a question?

4. After using these two word pictures, Jesus told the story of the prodigal son, one of His most famous parables. The story vividly illustrated the point He wanted the crowd to understand.

Why didn't Jesus simply tell this parable rather than start with the parables of the lost sheep and the lost coin?

5. Read Matthew 13:1–10. Notice that Jesus spoke to a large crowd, teaching them by using parables. In verse 10 the disciples questioned Jesus' method. Why do you think they asked this question?

6. Read Matthew 13:11–17. Why was Jesus teaching through parables?

7. Jesus more fully explained the parable of the sower in verse 18. But first He told the disciples something in verses 16 and 17. What did He say that caused them to listen intently to the explanation He was about to give?

8. Why is it imperative to wait until you have a person's attention before you tell him or her important information?

9. Based on Christ's examples, what is a good way to get someone's attention?

APPLICATION

Imagine that you want to teach an eleven-year-old boy honesty. He's lied several times lately, and you want to impress on him the importance of honesty. He doesn't care much about school, but he loves sports and cars. Use the Salt Principle we've discussed in this lesson and think up a story that would make him thirsty to learn about honesty.

TAPE

On the tape, we share how we use the Salt Principle in our family. Use this page for notes.

1. The Salt Principle is:

2. One way that it is misused is in:

3. To use the Salt Principle effectively:
    a.

    b.

    c.

    d.

e.

f.

COUPLE TALK

1. Ask your mate to share what topics get his or her attention most quickly.

2. Share with each other the times you feel most comfortable talking about important things as well as the times when you prefer not to talk about serious matters.

3. If you have children, discuss the following questions:

    a. What are two or three key concepts we want to teach them?

    b. What are their interests?

    c. How can we use the Salt Principle to communicate this information?

4. Work out a plan to use the Salt Principle with your child this week.

HOMEWORK

1. Schedule time to do Lesson 12 together (through Couple Talk, Part 1).

2. Use the Salt Principle with your children at least once this week.

12

Argue in Harmony

Is it possible to have a marriage without angry, hostile arguments? Many people would say it can't be done. Yet we've found that by applying one biblical truth, verbal fights can become almost non-existent in a marriage. This principle also tends to relieve disagreements with children and allows you to enjoy a more consistent spirit of harmony with every family member.

To experience this harmony, you'll need to invest some time. However, that investment pays tremendous dividends.

1. Read Philippians 1:27–28. What kind of conduct does Paul consider to be "worthy of the gospel of Christ"?

2. What advantages does the church have when it follows this instruction?

3. Read Philippians 2:1–2. What would cause Paul to say that his joy was complete?

4. What does Philippians 2:3–4 tell us about how to fulfill the command of verse 2?

5. How could these principles in Philippians help a marriage?

6. Using 1 Corinthians 1:10 as a guide, write your own definition of oneness in a marriage and family.

7. What does Proverbs 19:2 tell us about making decisions?

8. How can this principle apply in marriage and family relationships?

9. Look up the following verses in Proverbs. What principles can you find that will help you make family decisions?

Proverbs 1:5

Proverbs 11:14

Proverbs 12:15

COUPLE TALK (PART 1)

1. Complete this question by writing down a decision that you need to make as a couple:

Should we _____ ?

2. Under the YES column below and on the next page, write down all the reasons why you should pursue this course of action. Under the NO column, write all the reasons you should not.

YES	NO

3. Do you need any other facts? If so, write them down and decide where to obtain them.

4. Can you agree on the decision? If not, continue your discussion after you listen to the tape with your group.

TAPE

The principle of oneness, combined with the other principles you've learned in this study, can make your family so strong that almost nothing can destroy it. Listen now as we explain how this final principle works for us. Use this page for your notes.

1. Determine that you will never make an important family decision unless:

2. Gather all the facts before making a decision.

3. Evaluate each fact in light of _____ versus _____ factors.

4. Use contracts when necessary to help follow through on decisions you make.

COUPLE TALK (PART 2)

1. Using the chart on the next page, continue the discussion you started in Couple Talk, Part 1. Write out what you will lose or gain if you decide yes. Then write out what you will lose or gain if you decide no. After you have written down all the facts, put an "E" or a "T" after each item, identifying it as either an eternal or temporal factor.

2. Count up the eternal and temporal factors for both the loss and gain columns. Try to base your decision on the eternal value of your choices. If you both agree, the decision is made.

3. If you are still not in agreement, you need to continue to discuss the item—perhaps not at this moment—until you resolve it and agree on a direction. You may need to use some of the other principles taught in this study, such as gaining understanding through word pictures or open and closed spirits.

MAKING IMPORTANT FAMILY DECISIONS

What will we lose or gain if we decide yes?

LOSE   GAIN

What will we lose or gain if we decide no?

LOSE   GAIN

HOMEWORK

1. If you have children, schedule a family council to draw up a family contract. Choose one area of need, such as chores or neatness or how much time is spent watching TV. Allow everyone to have input. Draw up a contract based on that input. When everyone agrees, have each person sign the contract and mount it in a conspicuous place, like the refrigerator.

2. If you do not have children, schedule a time for just the two of you to talk about how to implement this principle in your marriage.

3. Schedule a time within the next month to review what you have learned in this study and to evaluate your progress as a couple.